The Soles of Your Feet

By Genichiro Yagyu

Translated by Amanda Mayer Stinchecum

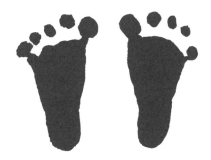

A CURIOUS NELL BOOK

Kane/Miller Book Publishers

Brooklyn, New York & La Jolla, California

The soles of my feet are much smaller than grandpa's.

A baby's feet are about this size.

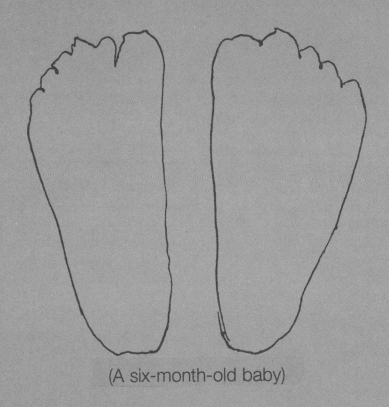

(A six-month-old baby)

To trace the soles of your feet, first put your left foot down on a piece of paper. Then, follow the edge of your foot with a pencil.

Now, put your right foot down on the paper and do the same thin

How big are your feet? Trace them here
(or, if you'd rather, on a separate piece of paper).

They should look like this.

with the soles of your feet.

→

If your drawing came out well, give yourself a hand

It's easier if you lie on your back.

A horse's foot is called a hoof.
The bottom of a horse's hoof is about this size.

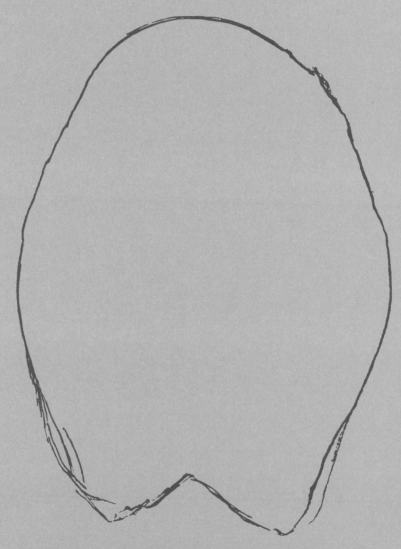

Here is a thoroughbred's hoof-print.
This horse weighs nearly 900 pounds.

The bottom of a horse's hoof
looks something like this.

This is the footprint of
my friend with the biggest
feet I know. He weighs
over 200 pounds.

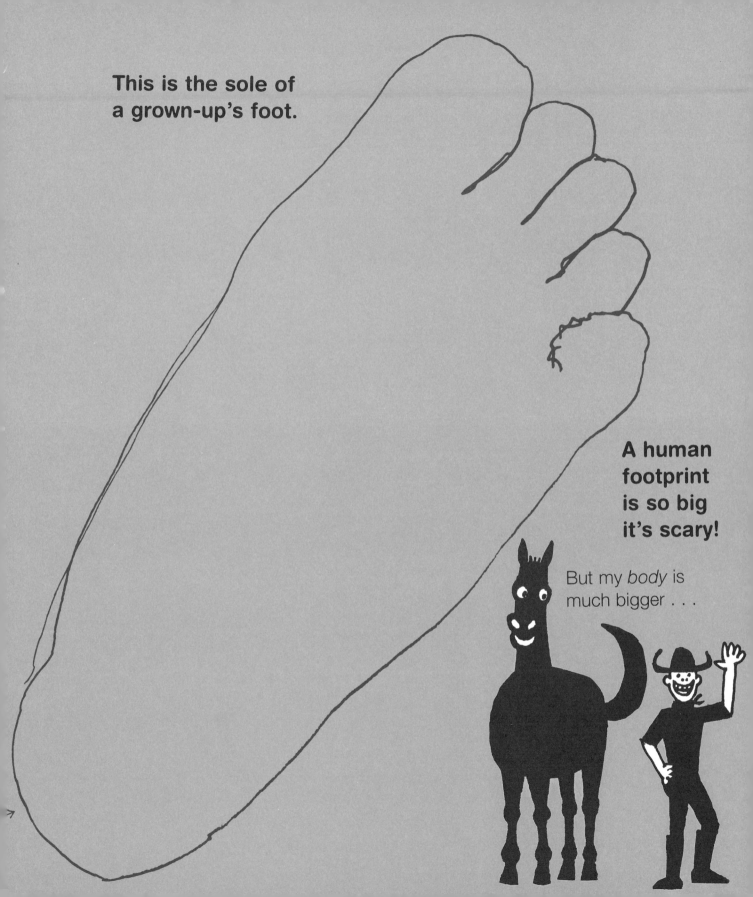

This is the sole of
a grown-up's foot.

**A human
footprint
is so big
it's scary!**

But my *body* is
much bigger . . .

We can do all sorts of things
with the soles of our feet.

We can even do things like this.

We also feel all kinds of things with the soles of our feet.

The grass feels good brushing against the soles of our feet.

On the hot, sandy beach . . . the bottoms of our feet burn! Yikes!

In the dark hallway, I just stepped on something.

What could it be?
Wait a second.
I'll try and guess.
It feels like . . . like
. . . a rubber band.

Right!

What's on the bottoms of your feet?

Nothing at all.

Really? Take a good look.

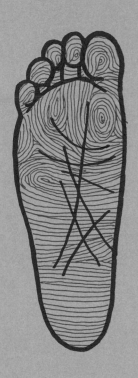

The soles of your feet are covered with fine lines that form a pattern, just like the palms of your hands.

These lines on the bottoms of your feet, like the ones on your hands, help you to sense what something feels like.

They also keep you from slipping . . . just as the ribbing on the bottoms of your sneakers or the tread on tires prevents slipping.

18.5

Now let's look at the soles of a gorilla's feet.

Hey, Mr. Gorilla, show us the bottoms of your feet.

BE MY GUEST.

The bottoms of a gorilla's feet and the palms of its hands are very similar.

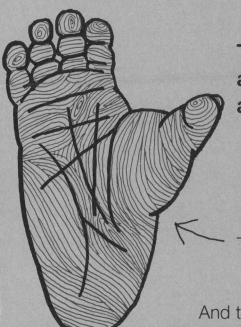

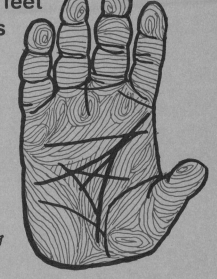

This is the sole of its foot.

And this is the palm of its hand.

The soles of *our* feet and the palms of *our* hands are different from each other. But in some ways they are similar.

Both have five fingers or toes. Also, both have fine lines that form a pattern.

Yes, I guess they are pretty much alike . . .

Then again, our toes are shorter than our fingers, and our big toes are in line with our other toes.

Hmmm, they really are different . . .

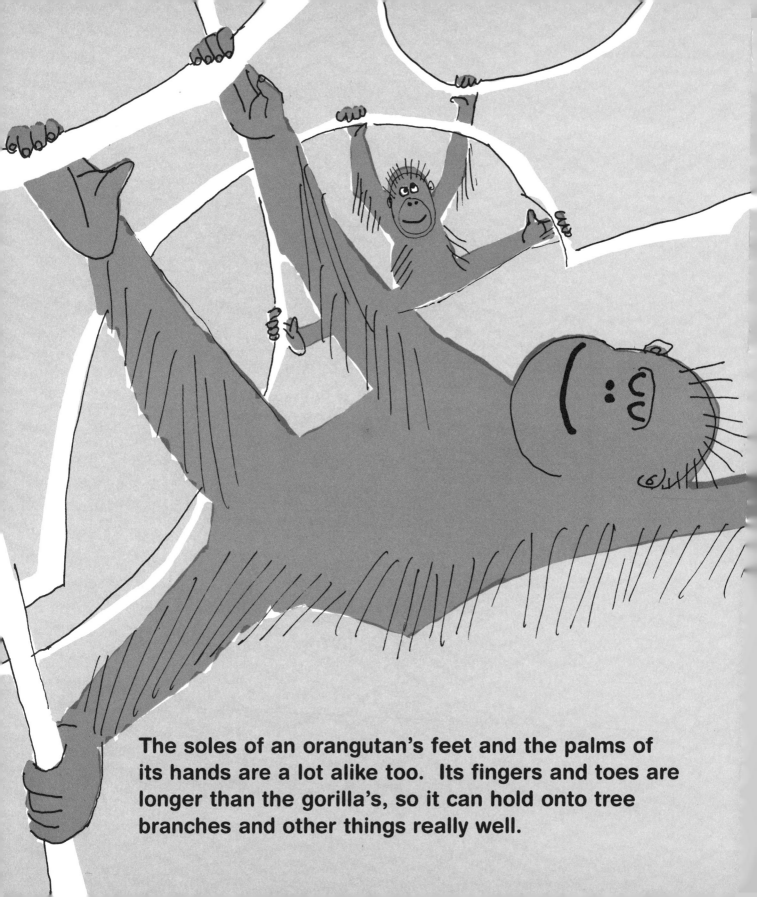

The soles of an orangutan's feet and the palms of its hands are a lot alike too. Its fingers and toes are longer than the gorilla's, so it can hold onto tree branches and other things really well.

Our toes aren't as long as an orangutan's, and they don't move as well, either.

But they can grab hold of little things, like a pencil or an eraser.

Can _you_ do this?

Aargh! Aargh!
In the old, old, old, old days, our ancestors, they say,
lived in treetops . . . something like this.
In those days, the soles of their feet were very much
like the palms of their hands.

Then, after a long, long time had passed,
our ancestors came down from the trees.
They stood on the ground, walked, ran, fell down.
And as they did, little by little, the soles of their
feet, that originally were like the palms of
their hands, changed and became like the
soles of *our* feet today.

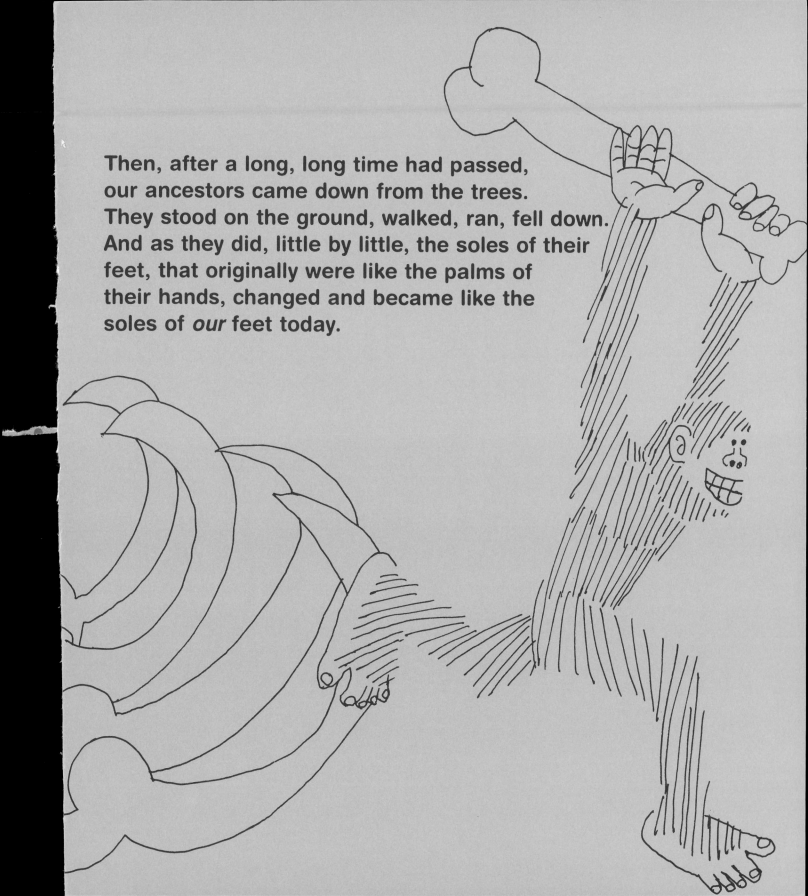

When we run, the bottoms of our feet touch the ground like this.

Watch carefully. The bottom of his right foot is about to hit the ground.

Look! His heel hit the ground first.

Then the rest of his foot follows . . .

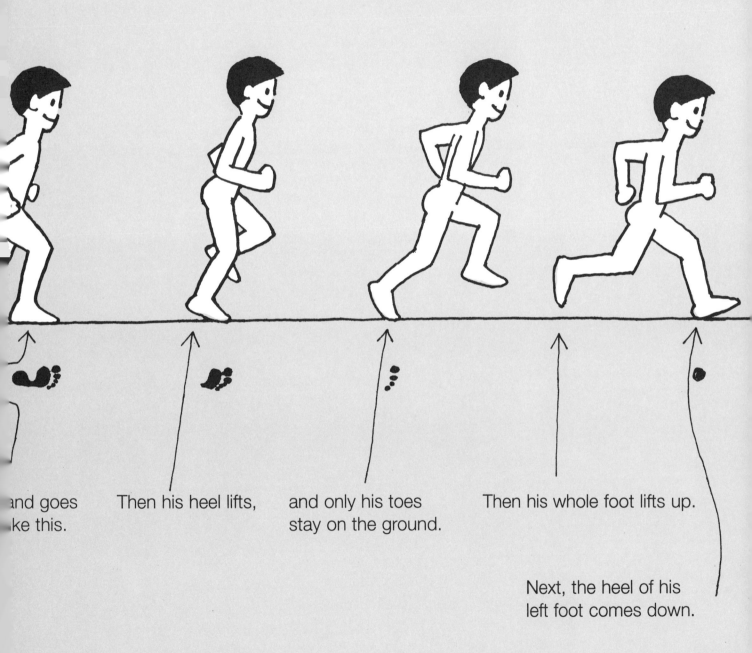

and goes like this.

Then his heel lifts,

and only his toes stay on the ground.

Then his whole foot lifts up.

Next, the heel of his left foot comes down.

Even when we put our whole foot flat on the ground, all of the sole doesn't touch.

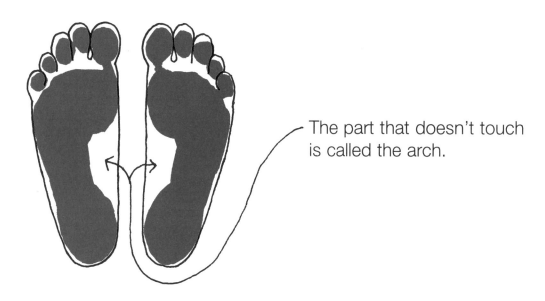

The part that doesn't touch is called the arch.

Some people have high arches; some have low ones.

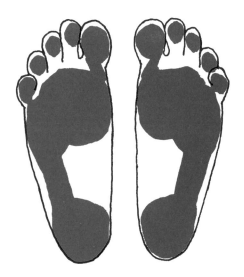

This person has high arches.

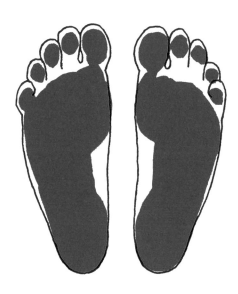

This person doesn't really have much of an arch.

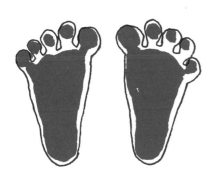

These feet have no arches at all.

They belong to a baby who can't walk yet.

When we are babies, we don't have any arches.
But when we start to walk, our arches develop little by little.

In general, people who walk a lot have high arches and strong legs. They can walk a long way without getting tired.

That doesn't mean that people with low arches are hopeless.

Even if they don't have much of an arch, they too can walk a long way. It just may be more tiring, but there's nothing to worry about.

What kind of arches do you have? Take a look at them.

It's easy to check. Paint the soles of your feet with paint
(make sure it's a kind you can wash off with water) and press them
down flat on the opposite page (or on a separate piece of paper).

I'm using red paint.

If there's some
paint left over,
try taking someone
else's footprints.